AIRB

COLIN ADDISON

LONDON
IAN ALLAN LTD

First published 1991

ISBN 0 7110 1988 6

© Ian Allan Ltd 1991

Published by Ian Allan Ltd,
Shepperton, Surrey; and printed
by Ian Allan Printing Ltd at their
works at Coombelands in
Runnymede, England

Previous page:
**Mexican carrier La Tur
became the first operator of
an AI product when it took
delivery of its first A300B4-
622 in 1989, being a
secondhand aircraft originally
manufactured in 1983.
Registered F-ODTK, it was
joined by a newly-built
machine registered F-ODSX
later the same year.**
Airbus Industrie

Right:
**An A300 of Garuda –
Indonesian Airlines is pictured
at the holding point at Kai Tak
prior to departure for Jakarta.**
Lance Cole

INTRODUCTION

For many years the US aviation manufacturers almost totally dominated commercial aircraft sales to airlines of the western world. This position was consolidated after World War 2 when European manufacturers were busy developing military hardware. The US planemakers developed refined versions of military transports which became the mainstay of major airline operations for almost two decades. Boeing, Douglas and Lockheed enjoyed market domination almost unchallenged with products including the Constellation, Stratocruiser and the DC-6/7 series. Realisation by European manufacturers of the market potential eventually resulted in innovative design of the first jet airliner and the first turboprop airliners. The Comet jetliner enjoyed limited success, mainly on the 'home' market, but with the Boeing 707 and Douglas DC-8 on the drawing board the already established US manufacturers were not seriously threatened by the type and American domination was maintained.

When the widebody era arrived it was once again the USA who led the field with the Boeing 747, Douglas DC-10 and Lockheed TriStar. During the late 1960s several European aircraft manufacturers gathered to discuss the possibility of a joint airliner project aimed at capturing a slice of the growing market for new generation jetliners. Only combined development, production and resources could possibly give a European project any real chance of market success. Major participants in the Airbus programme during the early stages were France, Germany and the British, although in traditional fashion, the British government withdrew support. The consortium which became Airbus Industrie started with a single product designated A300B. Interest by the British government towards the aerospace industry has always defied

Seen against a typical Austrian backdrop is Austrian Airlines'
A310-324ET, OE-LAB, sporting the temporary French markings
F-WWCK, this particular aircraft being the second of four on order.
Austrian has chosen a 172-seat configuration comprising 12 first
class, 37 business class and 123 economy seats.
Airbus Industrie

sensible reasoning, although on this occasion it looked as though they were right to withdraw as the initial market response to the Airbus was, to say the least, poor. During the first 10 years a grand total of 20 aircraft were sold plus one further machine on lease. Meanwhile, the US manufacturers had recorded sales in excess of 3,000 for their noisy, narrow-body products which included the Boeing 727, 737 and McDonnell Douglas DC-9. Airbus Industrie (AI) was almost defeated by European airlines and even the European media, who were less than enthusiastic about the product.

Across the Atlantic, the Americans were also doing their best to destroy market confidence in the Airbus. It has to be said that the Americans are great sports as long as they win although any threat to their own success is often dealt an underhand blow. Airline executives were reluctant to invest in a 'one-off' product from an unknown manufacturer and the consortium almost gave up in 1976 when only one aircraft was sold during the entire year. Today, AI has reached the pinnacle of manufacturing excellence and its product line is considered by many to be the finest in the world. The success of the Airbus stable consisting of the A300, A310 and A320 is likely to be continued when the A330 and A340, currently in the development stages, enter full production. Already commitments for the latter two variants have almost reached the 300 mark and the types have yet to fly!

The dramatic change of company fortunes came about simply because the A300 exceeded all expectations in terms of performance, operating costs and despatch reliability. As the number of aircraft in service steadily grew, so did the reputation of the consortium and today products from AI have penetrated the difficult North American market in substantial numbers, causing concern amongst US planemakers who — for far too long — had everything their own way.

Efficiency has been the deciding factor which has given AI such a commanding position on the world market. The flexibility of the original A300 design has proved its potential for range-stretch and in its latest variant as the 600 series it has a range of 4,400nm with sector reserves. Even greater range is offered by the derived A310-300 which is capable of 5,000nm sectors and is perhaps the most efficient airliner ever produced. Customers for the A300 have been able to specify their engine requirements as the underwing pylons can be aerodynamically modified for the entire range of CF6, JT9D and PW4000 series engines.

Final assembly of the Airbus is carried out at Toulouse where the various components arrive from consortium plants throughout Europe. Major contractors are British Aerospace, MBB, Aérospatiale, Fokker, CASA and Messier, with powerplants supplied by General Electric or Pratt & Whitney. Airbus Industrie operates a fleet of four Super Guppy freighters which collect components from the various sites for transportation to Toulouse. After assembly and initial flight-testing from Toulouse, the aircraft are flown to Hamburg/Finkenwerder for internal furnishing and seat installation.

From a single product base, AI announced the A310 variant at the Hanover airshow in West Germany during 1978. Initial interest in the A310 from Lufthansa and Swissair resulted in a joint design specification from both operators and the original concept was refined considerably by the time Swissair ordered 10 aircraft in early 1979. Lufthansa's order for an initial batch of 10 aircraft followed soon afterwards. Today, Lufthansa operates the A300, A310 and A320 along with firm orders for the A321 (stretched A320) and the A340. Swissair recently endorsed its commitment to the Airbus project with orders for seven A320s and 19 A321s, plus 26 options.

In an effort to broaden its product range, AI decided to develop a much smaller airliner which became known as the A320. The A300 and A310 established a broad market throughout the world and were identified as widebody jetliners with many common design features. The A320, however, is a narrow-bodied single-aisle design developed as a direct contender for the market enjoyed by such types as the Boeing 737 and 757. The A320 designation was first used in early 1981 but several stumbling blocks delayed further development for some months. AI became worried that, with production reaching saturation point at Toulouse, one of the other AI partners would have to be responsible for final production and flight-testing. Initially, BAe was considered, but possible political delays determined that facilities at Toulouse would be expanded to keep within AI's existing structure.

Another early problem was a suitable powerplant, although the CFM56 — which was at that time uncertified — was the obvious choice. Wrangling by potential customers over seat/price per mile figures continued to delay the project and it was not until 1984 that the A320 was truly launched. Without a doubt, the most significant advance of the A320 lies in the advanced digital flight control systems (fly-by-wire) design. The A320 flightdeck, designed by Porche Industries, differs considerably from earlier airliners, having no control yokes and very few traditional instruments. Each pilot has an unobstructed view of two large colour displays, with two more superimposed on the centreline. The onboard computer system of the A320 has been the subject of investigation following two crashes of the type involving an aircraft of Air France during an airshow sequence and an Indian Airlines example on a scheduled flight. Subsequent investigation has given the system a clean bill of health, renewing confidence in this revolutionary system. Air France was the launch customer for the A320, followed by commitments from British Caledonian (now transferred to British Airways) and Air Inter. The A320 first flew in February 1987 with a test-flight described by the crew as 'like a dream'. The first US breakthrough for the A320 occurred when Northwest decided to purchase the type. By 1992 Northwest will have 25 A320s in service. They have further endorsed AI products by placing orders for the A330 and A340. Since becoming launch customers for the A320 in the USA, Northwest has been joined by America West and Braniff, although the latter has now ceased operation.

For the future, AI has invested heavily in the development of its A330 twin, capable of carrying in the region of 350 passengers over sectors of up to 4,600nm, and the four-engined A340 with a range of up to 7,500nm. The UK will benefit considerably from the A330 project as the Rolls-Royce Trent 680 engine has been specified to power the type. Combined with the wing, the UK participation, by value, is almost 50% of the total cost. Only in the market slot occupied by the Boeing 747 does AI have no competitor aircraft. AI, once a poor relation to the huge US planemaking industry, is beating them at their own game. When Northwest placed its order for the A330 and A340 in 1987, a row broke out in Washington and all future Airbus orders within North America will now be closely scrutinised — a sure sign that the USA would like to dispense with competition when it becomes effective!

Operators of the various Airbus variants at the end of 1990 included:

Adria Airways; Alitalia; American Airlines; Air Afrique; Air Algerie; Air Canada; Air France; Air India; Air Inter; Air Jamaica; Air Liberte; Air Malta; Air Niugini; Air Portugal; Ansett Airlines; Australian Airlines; Austrian Airlines; Balair; British Airways; Canadian Airlines; China Airlines; China Eastern; Condor; Conair; Continental Airlines; Dan-Air; Eastern Airlines; Egyptair; Emirates Air Service; Garuda-Indonesian Airlines; Hapag Lloyd; Iberia; Indian Airlines; Interflug; Iran-Air; Japan Air Systems; Kar-Air; Kenya Airways; KLM – Royal Dutch Airlines; Korean Airlines; Kuwait Airways; Latur; Lufthansa; Malaysian Airlines System; Martinair; Monarch Airlines; Nigeria Airways; Northwest; Olympic; Pan American; Philippines Air Lines; Pakistan International; Royal Jordanian; SABENA – Belgian World Airlines; Singapore Airlines; Somali Airlines; South African Airways; Swissair; Trans European; Thai International; THY – Turkish Airlines; Tunis Air; United Arab Emirates Royal Flight; VASP; Viasa; ZAS – Airlines of Egypt.

New Airbus customers with deliveries expected from 1991 onward include:

Aerocancun; Aeroflot; All Nippon Airways; America West Airlines; Cathay Pacific; Compass Airlines; CSA; Gulf Air; LACSA; Mexicana; Trans World Airlines; UTA. Deliveries to Iraqi Airways were suspended following the Gulf War.

Top left:

British charter carrier Monarch Airlines received the first of four Airbus A300B4-605Rs in March 1990, becoming the first UK operator of the variant. Monarch had two aircraft in service for the 1990 IT season, flying from Luton and Gatwick to popular Mediterranean sunspots. The aircraft are operated in a high-density configuration with 361 economy seats. Powered by General Electric CF6-80C2A5 engines, the first aircraft registered G-MONR is shown at the holding point for runway 08 at Gatwick during September 1990.
Colin Addison, Kodachrome 64, 85mm lens 500sec/f5.6

Bottom left:

Emirates operates four Airbus A300B4-605Rs on nonstop services to several European destinations from its base at Dubai. The fleet also includes two A310-304s with a further three aircraft on order for delivery during 1992/93. Illustrated is the second A300 delivered to the carrier, registered A6-EKD, which operates in a 223-seat configuration with 18 first class, 42 business class and 163 economy seats.
Colin Addison, Kodachrome 64, 85mm lens 500sec/f5.6

Left:

Alitalia's A300B4-203, I-BUSB *Tiziano*, was delivered to the airline in 1980 and became the first of 14 to enter service. Twenty A320-100s are on order for delivery commencing during 1994.

Colin Addison, Kodachrome 64, 135mm lens 500sec/f5.6

Top right:

Kuwait Airways A300B4-620, 9K-AHG *Wara*, is one of three purchased by the airline for services around the Gulf and to destinations in Europe. The company also operates five A310-222s in a fleet which includes the Boeing 727, 747 and 767. Several of the Kuwaiti fleet were seized when Iraq invaded the country in August 1990.

Colin Addison, Kodachrome 64, 105mm lens 500sec/f5.6

Bottom right:

Air Jamaica's livery reflects the colourful atmosphere of the Caribbean and seems particularly well-suited to its fleet of four A300B4-203s. Amongst destinations served by Air Jamaica is Miami, Florida, where this Airbus was photographed lining-up for departure on runway 12 for a flight to Kingston.

Colin Addison, Kodachrome 64, 135mm lens 500sec/f5.6

Early morning arrival: An A300B4-203 of Air France crosses the threshold of runway 25L at Frankfurt/Main. The A300 wing has remained unchanged from early production aircraft through to the latest long-range 600 series variant. The deep design enabled AI to increase fuel capacity without any change to the external size of the wing. Clearly visible are the wide-chord tabbed Fowler flaps with two sections outboard of the engine pylon and one inboard. When fully extended this flap arrangement increases chord by 25%.

Colin Addison, Kodachrome 64, 85mm lens 500sec/f4.5

Above:

**Air France A300B4-203, F-BVGS, was delivered to the airline in
1981, being one of 16 in service. The company has ordered seven
long-range A340s for delivery commencing in 1994.**

Colin Addison, Kodachrome 64, 135mm lens 500sec/f5.6

Above:

Viasa of Venezuela operates a fleet comprising solely of wide-body aircraft, including three A300B-203s. YV-160C was built in 1977 for Lufthansa as D-AIBA and is currently leased from Guinness Peat Aviation. Viasa flights to Miami are operated by either A300 or DC-10 aircraft, where this shot was taken on the approach to runway 30.

Colin Addison, Kodachrome 64, 135mm lens 500sec/f5.6

Above:
**Iberia A300s were seen at several UK provincial airports during
1987 operating IT flights to Spanish resorts for UK tour operators.
Leeds/Bradford was amongst those served on a weekly basis.
Shown is EC-DNQ *Islas Cies*, built in 1981.**
Colin Addison, Kodachrome 64, 50mm lens 250sec/f8

Right:
**Iberia's scheduled flights into London-Heathrow are operated by a
variety of types, although the A300 features strongly. The Spanish
operator chose Pratt & Whitney JT9D-59A powerplants for its fleet,
including EC-DLG *Las Tablas de Daimiel*. Iberia has ordered A320,
A321 and A340 aircraft for its fleet modernisation programme.**
Colin Addison, Kodachrome 64, 1,000sec/f4.5

Although the 600 series looks like the very first A300B, it is in fact a very different aircraft, full of modern-day technical innovations. The fuselage features a rear section which is the same as the A310, the rear pressure bulkhead moved aft allowing a longer cabin which can be certified for up to 375 passengers. The first 600 flew in July 1983 with certification coming during the following year. First customer deliveries were to Saudia and Kuwait Airways. AI showed demonstrator F-WZLR at SBAC Farnborough in 1984.

Colin Addison, Kodachrome 64, 50mm lens 250sec/f5.6

Above:

AI sold A300s to Scandinavian Airlines Systems but that carrier disposed of the type in favour of US-built products. SAS subsidiary Scanair operated several A300B4s on IT flights during the early 1980s, including SE-DFL seen here on approach to Palma's Son San Juan airport.

Colin Addison, Kodachrome 64, 135mm lens 500sec/f5.6

Right:
The Airbus line carries the standard LD3 cargo containers compatible with all other wide-body airliners. Here an American Airlines A300B4-605R 'Luxury Liner' is made ready for a scheduled departure from Miami International.
Colin Addison, Kodachrome 64, 50mm lens 125sec/f5.6

Top left:
Egypt Air operates the A300B4-203 and the A300B4-622R — the latter on extended range operations (EROPS). The company took delivery of SU-GAR during 1990 when this photograph was taken, showing the burgundy and gold livery to advantage. Egypt Air has ordered a substantial number of A320s and A321s for fleet modernisation.
Colin Addison, Kodachrome 64, 135mm lens 500sec/f5.6

Bottom left:
First flown in June 1973 as the very first A300B2, F-BUAD has seen 17 years of continuous development flying with AI. Painted the striking house colours of AI, the aircraft was photographed at SBAC Farnborough. During the summer of 1990 the aircraft was noted at the desert airfield of Mojave, California, still actively engaged on hot weather trials.
Colin Addison, Kodachrome 64, 50mm lens 250sec/f8

Top right:

Lufthansa's A300B4-603, D-AIAR, was delivered to the company in early 1990 and is shown on approach to runway 27R at London-Heathrow.
Colin Addison, Kodachrome 64, 135mm lens 500sec/f4.5

Bottom right:

The Eastern Airlines order for the A300 was a coup for AI which sent shock waves throughout the US aviation industry. It was also the factor which changed the minds of many airlines around the world and AI's order book significantly improved from that day on.
Colin Addison, Kodachrome 64, 135mm lens 500sec/f5.6

Above:

**Greek flag-carrier Olympic Airways was an early purchaser of the
A300 and now has eight A300B4-103s in service, including SX-BEH
manufactured in 1982, five years after the first entered Olympic
service.**

Colin Addison, Kodachrome 64, 135mm lens 500sec/5.6

Above:
Pan American added A300B4-203, N216PA, to its fleet during 1990, being a secondhand example acquired from Eastern Airlines. The Pan Am A300s are seldom seen in Europe, being used mainly for services within North America and to Central and South America.
Colin Addison, Kodachrome 64, 135mm lens 500sec/f5.6

Left:
Eastern Airlines' continued struggle to survive has resulted in substantial pruning of the company fleet. A number of A300s have been sold although N201EA was still in service during the summer of 1990.
Colin Addison, Kodachrome 64, 135mm lens 500sec/f5.6

Bottom left:
To the casual onlooker every other movement at Frankfurt/Main appears to be a product of the AI stable. Most prolific are the machines of Lufthansa operating from the airline's busy hub. Its A300B4-603s are used primarily to destinations in Africa and the Middle East, although some high-density routes within Europe are served. Here, D-AIAI *Erbach/Odenwald* is prepared for a night departure from Frankfurt.
Colin Addison, Kodachrome 64, 50mm lens 6sec/f5.6

Right:
German charter operator Hapag Lloyd was an operator of the A300 although it has now disposed of the type in favour of the A310. Illustrated is D-AHLC on final approach to Palma airport.
Colin Addison, Kodachrome 64, 135mm lens 500sec/f5.6

Top right:
Known formerly as Garuda Indonesian Airways, Garuda Indonesian is the state-owned national airline of Indonesia with an extensive passenger and cargo network radiating from the hub of Jakarta.

Amongst other types, the airline operates nine A300B4-200s which offer increased range with greater fuel capacity and higher weights than the B2 variant.

Garuda's A300B4, PK-GAC, is pictured having just taken off from Hong Kong's Kai Tak airport on 8 December 1987. *Robbie Shaw*

Bottom right:
During the latter part of the 1980s, the US carrier Eastern Airlines was plagued by a series of ruinous financial and labour problems which resulted in the airline filing for Chapter 11 bankruptcy protection during 1989. Asset sales and the disposal of routes were undertaken in a bid to stem the decline and reshape the ailing airline. At the time this photograph was taken at Miami on 27 May 1990, Eastern had a fleet of 20 A300B4s. *Robbie Shaw*

Above:
Continental's A300B4, N968C, is pushed back from its stand at Newark, New Jersey, on 25 May 1990, while on the flightdeck the crew run through their pre-start-up checklist before preparing to bring the main engines to life. In the background can be seen a Boeing 747SP of United Airlines. *Robbie Shaw*

Far left:
Only a few brief seconds before its main gear kisses the tarmac of Miami airport, Continental's A300B4-203 whistles in over the approach lights, silhouetted against the dramatic backdrop of a Turneresque evening sky. *Aviation Picture Library/Austin J. Brown*

Top left:
Passenger transport, then and now: a Douglas DC-3, backbone of the world's airlines and military transport fleets for several decades since the 1930s, crouches in the foreground as Eastern's A300B4-203, N221EA, whines past on the taxiway at Miami during March 1985. *Aviation Picture Library/Austin J. Brown*

Bottom left:
One of the world's largest domestic carriers, Indian Airlines operates scheduled services to over 70 cities in India and abroad from four centres at Delhi, Bombay, Madras and Calcutta. A300s and A320s form the greater part of its fleet, with more A320s on order at the time of writing.
Indian Airlines' A300B2, VT-EDZ, is pictured during a turnaround, while in the background can be seen an Antonov An-12 'Cub' four-turboprop freighter, typifying the interesting mix of eastern and western aircraft types to be found on the sub-continent. *Aviation Picture Library/Charles Tyler*

Japan Air System's A300, JA8263, is steered smoothly on to the runway threshold to await final take-off clearance from Osaka tower on 19 April 1990. *Robbie Shaw*

Air Afrique is the international carrier for 10 independent African countries operating an extensive network of services in Africa and to a number of European destinations.

A300B4-203, TU-TAO, is one of three A300s operated by the carrier and is pictured at Paris-Charles de Gaulle airport in March 1983. *Aviation Picture Library/Austin J. Brown*

Resplendent in the bright livery of the Colombian carrier Aerocondor Colombia, A300B4-103, HK-2057, is pictured at San Juan, Puerto Rico, during April 1979. *Aviation Picture Library/Austin J. Brown*

Eastern's A300B4-103, N205EA, takes off into a stormy Barbadian sky in December 1982, 'headin' stateside'. During 1989, Eastern sold its South American and Caribbean routes to its rival, American Airlines, before being accepted into Chapter 11 bankruptcy protection. *Aviation Picture Library/Austin J. Brown*

Above:

Only in the market sector occupied by the Boeing 747, AI cannot field a competitor. In all other areas the consortium is giving Boeing direct competition with a major market breakthrough on the US giant's home ground. Shown in this night study at Frankfurt are an A310-300 of Emirates and a Boeing 747-200 of South African Airways.

Colin Addison, Fuji 64 Tungsten, 85mm lens 6sec/f5.6

Above:
Cyprus Airways operates a mixed fleet including four A310-203s alongside A320s and BAC One-Elevens. Scheduled services to the UK centre on London-Heathrow, whilst IT charters loaded with sunseekers operate from many provincial airports to Larnaca.
Colin Addison, Kodachrome 64, 105mm lens 500sec/f4.5

Above:
Cyprus Airways operated IT flights from Leeds/Bradford airport for the first time during 1990, offering a combined service from Leeds and Newcastle to Larnaca on behalf of Cypriana Holidays. All flights were operated by A310s, including 5B-DAR.

Top left:
Delivery of THY A310-204s commenced in 1985 and by late 1990 13 of an order for 14 had entered service. The company uses the type on services to Europe, the Far East and plans to utilise the fleet for flights to the USA.
Colin Addison, Kodachome 64, 135mm lens 500sec/f5.6

Bottom left:
This THY – Turkish Airlines A310 appears to be smiling as it rests before a flight from Frankfurt to Istanbul.
Colin Addison, Kodachrome 64, 300mm lens 250sec/f8

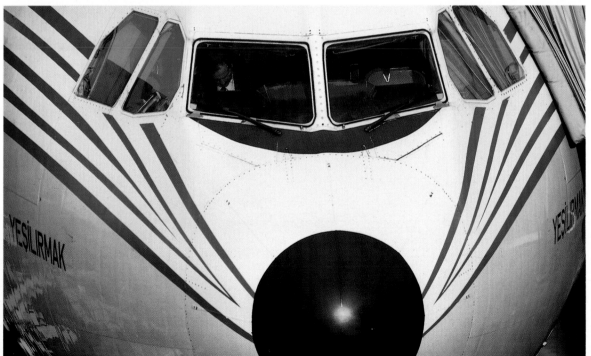

Air India was among the early operators of the A310-300. A310-300, VT-ESG, *Yahuna*, is one of some 11 Airbuses operated by the carrier in mid-1991 and is pictured here at Kai Tak airport. *Robbie Shaw*

Right:
Pan American's fleet of A310s are used extensively on services from North America to Europe. Here, *Clipper Mayflower* pulls up to the gate at Frankfurt after the long journey from Detroit.
Colin Addison, Kodachrome 64, 85mm lens 125sec/f5.6

Top left:

Swissair and Lufthansa collaborated in a joint design specification for the A310, resulting in an order for 10 aircraft by Swissair in 1979. Swissair further endorsed the AI product line in 1990 by placing an order for 26 assorted A320/321s. The fourth aircraft, registered HB-IPD, was delivered to Swissair in 1983 and is shown on finals at London-Heathrow.
Colin Addison, Kodachrome 64, 135mm lens 500sec/f5.6

Bottom left:

Despite operating a fleet of mainly US-manufactured types, KLM — Royal Dutch Airlines has 10 A310-203s in service on routes within Europe and to the Middle East.
Colin Addison, Kodachrome 64, 105mm lens 500sec/f5.6

Royal Jordanian Airlines (formerly Alia) operates six A310-304s in the company's strikingly elaborate livery. All six aircraft carry French markings, including F-ODVG *Prince Faisal*, seen on approach to Frankfurt.
Colin Addison, Kodachrome 64, 105mm lens 500sec/f5.6

Left:

Night scene at Frankfurt/Main with Emirates A310-304, A6-EKA, on the gate whilst Royal Jordanian A310, F-ODVH, is pushed back for departure to Amman. The A310 has enjoyed considerable success since it flew for the first time on 3 April 1982. Originally envisaged as a short/medium-range transport by AI, airline pressure for a longer-range aircraft as a suitable replacement for Boeing 707s and DC-8s resulted in the definitive 300 series variant.
Colin Addison, Fuji 64 tungsten, 85mm lens 6 secs/f5.6

Overleaf:

Pan American's A310s fly routes from North America to Europe where traffic loads do not justify the use of Boeing 747s. The type is a true wide-body, offering spacious accommodation, with this particular aircraft fitted out in a mixed 192-seat configuration.
Colin Addison, Kodachrome 64, 50mm lens 125sec/f5.6

Top left:

TAP – Air Portugal's attractive red and green livery is shown to advantage in this shot of A310-304, CS-TEW, which was delivered to the company in early 1990.
Colin Addison, Kodachrome 64, 135mm lens 500sec/f5.6

Bottom left:

D-AICA was the first A310 for Lufthansa, delivered to the company in 1982. Like many airlines, Lufthansa has now adopted a simplified livery consisting of a fuselage devoid of a cheatline. This particular aircraft was still resisting adoption of the new scheme when photographed at Frankfurt in November 1990. An almost monochrome effect was attained by shooting the aircraft against the sinking sun on a cold, damp evening.
Colin Addison, Kodachrome 64, 300mm lens 250sec/f5.6

Top right:
**Lufthansa experimented with
several colour scheme
variations during the late
1980s before this somewhat
bland livery was finally
adopted. In its systems, the
A310 basically follows the
A300 although it employs a
digital automatic flight control
system. This enables
computer flight guidance,
including stability
augmentation and thrust
control, suitable for Cat II
landings.**
*Colin Addison, Kodachrome 64,
135mm lens 500sec/f5.6*

Bottom right:
**Pictured on finals at London-
Gatwick airport on 13 January
1991, Emirates' A310-300,
A6-AKE, is one of two
operated by the airline,
although most of the
destinations served by the
airline are in the Middle and
Far East.**
      **Emirates is a relative
newcomer to the world's
airline scene, having only
begun operations in October
1988.** *Robbie Shaw*

In 1984, CAAC (The Civil Aviation Administration of China) was dismantled to create several regional carriers, each with varying degrees of autonomy, while Air China has operated on international services since July 1988. To assist in its route network expansion, Air China placed a US $850 million order for Boeing 747s, 767s and Airbus A310s in May 1986.

CAAC-affiliated airlines have a large and varied fleet of aircraft which includes three A310-200s and two A310-300s, exemplified here by A310-300, B-2305, seen at Kai Tak airport on 13 December 1987. *Robbie Shaw*

Far left:
Toronto turnaround: two of Wardair Canada's A310-300s receive attention from the ground servicing crews on 29 May 1989. In the foreground can be seen C-FNWD *Jack Moar*. **During early 1990, Wardair Canada ceased to exist as an independent airline, its operations being absorbed by the giant Canadian Airlines International.** *Robbie Shaw*

Top left:
Double vision: awaiting clearance from the tower for take-off from London-Heathrow's runway 27L, Swissair's A310-200, HB-IPA, is followed by another company A310, HB-IPE, and a British Airways Boeing 737-200, on 25 April 1990. During 1990, Swissair's fleet included five A310-200s and four A310-300s. *Robbie Shaw*

Bottom left:
The Portuguese carrier TAP-Air Portugal operates an extensive network of scheduled passenger and freight services with a mixture of Airbus Industrie, Boeing and Lockheed aircraft types. The airline currently (mid-1991) operates five A310-300s and has two of the four-engined A340s on order for delivery in 1992/93.
   Pictured here at Frankfurt-Main airport on 21 May 1989 is TAP's A310-300, CS-TEJ. *Robbie Shaw*

Above:

Lufthansa is one of the largest customers for the A320, with 31 aircraft on order with 18 delivered by the end of 1990. The first flight of the type occurred in 1987 and customer deliveries began in 1988 with examples for Air France, Air Inter and British Caledonian.

Colin Addison, Kodachrome 64, 85mm lens 2secs/f5.6

Right:

British Airways adopted the A320 fleet ordered by British Caledonian and has commented favourably about the introduction of the type into the BA fleet. All 10 aircraft in the initial order had been delivered by late 1990. Illustrated is G-BUSF (note the lack of wing fences, since adopted by all new Airbus aircraft).

Colin Addison, Kodachrome 64, 300mm lens 1,000sec/f4.5

Right:
Lufthansa's A320s will be joined by the stretched A321 when initial deliveries to the airline begin in 1994. The airline is using the type on internal services and to destinations throughout Europe. Shown is D-AIPR on the approach to Frankfurt.
Colin Addison, Kodachrome 64, 135mm lens 500sec/f5.6

Top right:

Air Canada took delivery of the first of 38 A320s in January 1990, becoming the first operator of the type in Canada. The type serves destinations throughout Canada and across the border into the USA. Air Canada will eventually replace its Boeing 727s and DC-9s with the type. Illustrated is C-GDRK at Toronto International with a backdrop of Air Canada Boeing 747 and 767 aircraft.
Colin Addison, Kodachrome 64, 85mm lens 250sec/f8

Bottom right:

Air France took delivery of its first A320-111 in March 1988. The airline lost its third aircraft, registered F-GFKC, in a crash during an air show sequence at Mulhouse-Habsheim during June of the same year in which three passengers died. Almost two years later, Indian Airlines lost an A320 on the approach to Bangalore, killing 92 of the 156 persons on board. For different reasons, both these ill-fated aircraft were being flown too slowly and at too low an altitude before their respective pilots applied power and the aircraft sank into the ground. In both cases the A320 has been exonerated, with the accidents attributed to pilot error. Due to the advanced design features of the A320, these accidents had provided the media with ammunition to question the safety of placing so much reliance on computer controls.
Colin Addison, Kodachrome 64, 135mm lens 500sec/f5.6

Far right:

Arrival at dusk: an Air France A320 caught on the approach to runway 08 at London-Gatwick.
Colin Addison, Kodachrome 64, 300mm lens 1,000sec/f2.8

Far left:

Some of Royal Jordanian's shorter sector flights into Europe are operated by A320 aircraft. Frankfurt is amongst one of the airports served by the type. Like the A310s in the fleet, the A320s also sport French registrations, including F-OGYB.
Colin Addison, Kodachrome 64, 85mm lens 250sec/f5.6

Top left:

***Island of Sark*, registered G-BUSJ, was the ninth A320 to enter service with British Airways (note the wing fences which do not feature on all of the BA A320 fleet).**
Colin Addison, Kodachrome 64, 135mm lens 500sec/f5.6

Bottom left:

A320, G-BUSE, was delivered to British Airways in December 1988 and became *Isle of Scilly* in company service.
Colin Addison, Kodachrome 64, 300mm lens 1,000sec/f4

Far left:
Certification and flight-testing of the A320 involved four aircraft, all fitted initially with CFM56-5 turbofans produced by the General Electric/SNECMA partnership, although one A320-100 (F-WWAI) was retrofitted with V2500 engines produced by the International Aero Engines (IAE) consortium. Air France became the first operator of the A320. *Aviation Picture Library/Austin J. Brown*

Above:
Airbus Industrie's A320-100 demonstrator, F-WWAI, powered by two IAE V2500 turbofans, each developing between 23,500-25,000lb st at take-off, climbs steeply away from Farnborough's runway during the 1988 SBAC air show. The A320-100 and 200 are externally similar, although they differ in fuel capacities and operating weights. *Aviation Picture Library/Austin J. Brown*

FD

Lufthansa

Airbus A320-200
...en am Rhein

Saarbrücken

Above:

Lufthansa's A320s share the short-haul European routes with the company's Boeing 737-300s. Like the A320, the737-300 is also powered by the CFM56 turbofan, but it accommodates less passengers (149 to 179) in a six-abreast high-density configuration than the A320.

Lufthansa's A320-211, D-AIPL, is pictured at Düsseldorf airport in October 1990. *Aviation Picture Library/Austin J. Brown*

Back cover:

Shown to advantage on this shot of an Air France A300 B4-203 are the full-span leading edge slats arranged in three long slat sections with no break at the engine pylon. This seemingly perfect arrangement has been beneficial to operators serving high-altitude locations where performance is often compromised.
Colin Addison, Kodachrome 64, 300mm lens 1,000sec/f4.5